Apples

by Ann L. Burckhardt

Reading Consultant:
Julia Daly
International Apple Institute

Bridgestone Books
an Imprint of Capstone Press

Bridgestone Books are published by Capstone Press
818 North Willow Street, Mankato, Minnesota 56001
Copyright © 1996 by Capstone Press
Printed in the United States of America

Library of Congress Cataloging-in-Publication Data
Burckhardt, Ann, 1933-
    Apples/ by Ann L. Burckhardt
    p. cm.--(Early-reader science. Foods.)
    Includes bibliographical references (p.24) and index.
    Summary: Simple text introduces apples, and instructions are given for making an
apple pomander.
    ISBN 1-56065-448-1
    1.Apples--Juvenile literature. 2. Nature craft--Juvenile literature. [1.Apples.]
    I. Title. II. Series.
SF487.5.B735 1996
636.5--dc20

                         95-54167
                            CIP
                              AC

Photo credits
Unicorn/Martha McBride, cover; Joseph Fontenot, 12; Alice Prescott, 14.
International Stock, 4, 10, 20.
Michelle Coughlan, 6, 16.
FPG, 8.
Corbis-Bettmann, 18.

Table of Contents

Words in **boldface** type in the text are defined in the Words to Know section in the back of this book.

What Are Apples?

Apples are one of the most popular fruits. The world produces more than 2 billion **bushels** of apples every year. The average person eats 50 apples every year.

Different Kinds of Apples

There are more than 7,500 different kinds of apples. Some are grown to be sold in stores. These include McIntosh, Granny Smith, Delicious, Golden Delicious, and Rome.

Parts of an Apple

An apple has five main parts. They are the skin, **flesh**, core, seeds, and stem. The skin of an apple can be red, yellow, or green. The flesh of an apple can taste sweet or **tart**.

Where Apples Grow

Apples grow on an apple tree. They grow best in areas that have cool winters. During the winter, apple trees prepare for growing again. The state of Washington produces the most apples in North America.

How Apples Grow

In the spring, buds appear on apple tree branches. The buds grow leaves and then flowers. When the flowers die, green bulges start growing in their place. These bulges grow into apples.

Harvest

Apples are ready to **harvest** when they can be easily pulled off the tree. Harvesters pick the apples by hand. They use ladders to reach the high branches.

How We Use Apples

Apples are used to make many things. Apple cider, applesauce, and apple butter are made with apples. Eating an apple is very good for your teeth.

History

Pilgrims brought apples to North America. Presidents Washington and Jefferson both grew apple trees. Johnny Appleseed lived in the early 1800s. He walked from farm to farm planting apple seeds for many years.

Apples and People

People say an apple a day keeps the doctor away. They say some things are as American as apple pie. New York City is called the Big Apple.

Hands On: Make an Apple Pomander

A pomander is an air freshener made from fruit and cloves. In the past, pomanders were often used to freshen rooms.

You will need
- a firm apple
- fork
- ground cinnamon
- whole cloves
- bowl
- ribbon
- 8-inch (20-centimeter) square of nylon net

1. Use a fork to prick holes in the apple.
2. Push the stem of a whole clove into each hole.
3. Put the apple in a bowl. Sprinkle ground cinnamon on it.
4. Let the apple and bowl sit in a cool place for a few days.
5. Put the apple in the center of the nylon net.
6. Tie the top of the net with ribbon.
7. Hang or set the pomander in your room. It will smell sweet and fresh.

Words to Know

bushel—dry unit of measure equal to 32 quarts (35 liters), or about 100 apples

flesh—the edible part of a fruit or vegetable

harvest—gather a crop

tart—sharp sour taste

Read More

De Bourgoing, Pascale. *Fruit*. A First Discovery Book. New York: Scholastic, 1991.

Lindbergh, Reeve. *Johnny Appleseed*. Boston: Little, Brown, 1990.

Maestro, Betsy. *How Do Apples Grow?* New York: HarperCollins, 1992.

Micucci, Charles. *The Life and Times of the Apple*. New York: Orchard Books, 1992.

Index